Alaska Cruise Travel Guide 2025

Ketchikan Stop, Seaplane Excursion, Soaring Over The Misty Fjords National Monument, Clear lakes, And Towering Granite Cliffs, Local Delicacies.

By

Gladys J. Carron

Copyright © 2024 by Gladys J. Carron. All rights reserved.

No part of this publication may be reproduced, distributed, or transmitted in any form or by any means, including photocopying, recording, or other electronic or mechanical methods, without the prior written permission of the publisher, except in the case of brief quotations embodied in critical reviews and certain other non-commercial uses permitted by copyright law.

Disclaimer

The information contained in this guide is for general informational purposes only. While every effort has been made to provide accurate and up-to-date information, the publisher and author make no representations or warranties of any kind, express or implied, about the completeness, accuracy, reliability, suitability, or availability with respect to the guide or the information, products, services, or related graphics contained in the guide for any purpose. Any reliance you place on such information is therefore strictly at your own risk.

The publisher and author shall not be held responsible or liable for any loss or damage caused directly or indirectly by the use or misuse of the information contained in this guide, nor for any errors, omissions, or changes in information such as travel regulations, costs, schedules, or other specifics that may occur after publication.

All trademarks, product names, and company names or logos cited in this guide are the property of their respective owners.

Table of Contents

Chapter 1. Introduction — 6
    Welcome to Your Alaska Cruise Adventure — 6
    Why Choose an Alaska Cruise? — 8

Chapter 2. Planning Your Alaska Cruise — 12
    Best Time to Cruise — 12
    Choosing the Right Cruise Line and Ship — 15
    Shore Excursions & Itineraries — 19

Chapter 3. Cruise Itineraries — 24
    Common Routes and Ports of Call — 24
    Highlights of Each Port — 25
    Suggested Itineraries for Different Interests and Durations. — 32

Chapter 3. What to Pack — 36
    Essential Items to Pack for an Alaska Cruise — 36
    General Weather Tips — 40

Chapter 4. Onboard Experience — 42
    Accommodation Options — 42
    Dining and Cuisine — 48
    Entertainment and Activities — 54
    Kids' Clubs and Activities — 58

Chapter 5. Excursions and Activities — 62
    Popular Shore Excursions — 62
    Adventure Activities — 68
    Cultural Experiences: A Personal Journey — 70

Chapter 6. Wildlife and Nature — 73
    Key Wildlife to Look For — 73
    Best Times and Places for Wildlife Viewing — 77

Natural Landmarks and Scenic Highlights 81
Chapter 7. Tips for a Smooth Trip 88
Navigating the Cruise Terminal 88
Health and Safety Tips for Your Alaska Cruise 90
Budgeting and Saving Money 93
Chapter 8.Resources And Itineraries 97
Example Daily Schedule for a 7–10 Day Cruise 97
Tour operators' contact details 100
Bonus: Advice on Photography 102

Chapter 1. Introduction

Welcome to Your Alaska Cruise Adventure

Welcome aboard! I vividly recall the exhilaration of my first Alaska cruise, a vacation that would permanently reshape my sense of nature's grandeur and the spirit of adventure. As the ship set sail from the bustling harbor, excitement and anticipation raced within me. The huge, unbroken expanse of the Pacific spread out before us, promising wonders beyond conception.

The first evening, as we went by the rough coastline, the setting sun created a golden glow on the surrounding mountains, their peaks dusted with snow even in midsummer. I stood on the deck, a warm cup of cocoa in hand, the fresh sea breeze ruffling my hair. The air was filled with the aroma of sea and pine, an exhilarating blend that screamed of wild, untamed areas.

Our first point of call was Ketchikan, regarded as the "Salmon Capital of the World." Here, I embarked on a spectacular seaplane excursion, soaring over the Misty Fjords National Monument. From above, the area opened like a magnificent tapestry of verdant trees, clear lakes, and towering granite cliffs. The plane's descent brought us to a lonely lake, where we landed gently on the crystal water. Stepping out onto the float, I had a great sensation of solitude and connection with the wild.

Back on the ship, days were filled with adventure and evenings with comfort. The onboard dining was a revelation – fresh seafood, served to perfection, supplemented by local delicacies. One night, when we dined in a fine restaurant, I savored a meal of Alaskan king crab legs, their sweet, supple meat a testament to the richness of these seas.

The expedition continued via the Inside Passage, a labyrinth of islands and canals where animals abounded. I spent hours on deck with binoculars, observing humpback whales breaching in the distance, their gigantic bodies generating splashes that shone in the sunlight. Closer to shore, sea otters laid on their backs, breaking apart mussels, as bald eagles swooped above, their acute eyes scouring the ocean for prey.

Glacier Bay was a highlight, a location where time seemed to stand still. As our ship sailed the frigid seas, towering glaciers loomed all about, their dazzling blue hues a dramatic contrast against the grey sky. The sound of calving ice – large chunks breaking off and falling into the sea – rang across the fjords, a striking reminder of nature's raw, relentless powers. Standing on the deck, dressed up against the cold, I felt a sense of wonder and humility, observing the beauty of these ancient ice formations.

The cultural richness of Alaska was equally compelling. In Juneau, I visited the Alaska State Museum, where exhibits displayed the history and traditions of Alaska's indigenous peoples. Later, a visit to a Tlingit community brought a greater understanding of their way of life, as elders told stories passed down through generations.

Every day provided new thrills, from hiking through jungles to kayaking in quiet bays, from interacting with locals to relishing fresh catch right off the boat. By the end of the voyage, I was not just a passenger; I was a part of Alaska's story, a witness to her wild beauty and resilient spirit.

As you travel on your own Alaska cruise, know that you are about to visit a location where nature reigns supreme, where every turn offers spectacular views, and every minute is a chance to create wonderful memories. Welcome to Alaska, a land of limitless wonders and eternal adventures.

Alaska Adventure Sai

The Hot Bite
American

Alaska Cruise Adventure

Scan the QR code
1. Open Camera: Launch your smartphone's camera app.
2. Position QR Code: Place the QR code within the camera's viewfinder.
3. Hold Steady: Keep the device steady for the camera to focus.
4. Wait for Scan: Wait for the code to be recognized.
5. Tap Notification: Follow the prompt to access the content.

Why Choose an Alaska Cruise?

Alaska cruise is more than simply a holiday; it's a journey into some of the most pristine and awe-inspiring places on Earth. Here are compelling reasons why an Alaska cruise should be at the top of your travel list:

Alaska features some of the most spectacular scenery in the world. Imagine cruising by towering glaciers, snow-capped mountains, and lush, pristine woods. The magnificent fjords and clear waterways form a stunning backdrop for your voyage. Glacier Bay National Park, with its gigantic tidewater glaciers, and the Inside Passage, a network of picturesque rivers, offer landscapes that are unequaled.

An Alaska cruise is a wildlife enthusiast's dream. From the deck of your ship, you can observe humpback whales breaching, orcas gliding across the sea, and joyful dolphins riding the bow wave. On land trips, you might observe grizzly bears fishing for salmon, bald eagles flying above, and sea otters floating gently on their backs. The sheer diversity and richness of wildlife make every minute exhilarating.

Alaska cruises provide a selection of shore activities that cater to every interest. Whether you want to stroll through beautiful jungles, take a helicopter tour to a remote glacier, or kayak in tranquil coves, the alternatives are unlimited. Fishing outings, gold panning activities, and visits to historic cities like Skagway and Ketchikan add to the depth of the experience.

Alaska's indigenous cultures and history give an interesting depth to your journey. You'll get opportunities to visit Tlingit, Haida, and Tsimshian villages, where you may learn about traditional crafts, listen to stories, and watch cultural performances. Museums and historical sites throughout the region offer insights into Alaska's gold rush past and its maritime legacy.

An Alaska cruise blends the thrill of adventure with the luxury and convenience of a floating hotel. Modern cruise ships provide opulent amenities, from gourmet dining and spa services to spacious accommodations with magnificent vistas. You can explore isolated and untamed regions without sacrificing comfort, making it a great alternative for travelers of all ages and mobility levels.

Cruises generally provide exceptional value for your money, as many fees are covered in the package. Meals, hotels, entertainment, and transportation between places are all covered, making budgeting easy. Special packages and bargains can further increase affordability, delivering a high-quality experience without breaking the budget.

Whether you have a week or two weeks spare, there's an Alaska cruise itinerary that meets your schedule. From short tours focused on significant landmarks to extended cruises that explore deeper into distant places, you may choose an itinerary that meets your interests and time restrictions. Each journey is unique, offering distinct ports of call and experiences.

Unlike other remote travel destinations that could require substantial planning and several modes of transport, an Alaska cruise streamlines the logistics. You may begin from large towns like Seattle or Vancouver, making it easy to start your voyage. Once aboard, everything is taken care of, enabling you to focus on enjoying the ride.

Choosing an Alaska cruise is about embracing the spirit of discovery and amazement. It's about going into a world where nature's magnificence is on full display, where every day brings fresh discoveries and amazing encounters. Whether you're a seasoned traveler or going on your first big adventure, an Alaska cruise offers an experience that will leave you fascinated and craving for more.

Chapter 2. Planning Your Alaska Cruise

Best Time to Cruise

Choosing the optimum time to cruise to Alaska can considerably enhance your trip, since each part of the sailing season offers unique advantages. Here's a detailed look at what each time of year brings:

May: Early Season Charm

Weather and Scenery: May marks the beginning of the Alaska cruise season. The temperatures are colder, often ranging from the mid-40s to mid-50s Fahrenheit. Snow still crowns the mountains, and the landscape continues to awaken from winter, with flowering wildflowers adding dashes of color.

Wildlife: This is a fantastic time for bird watching as migrating species return to the region. You might also witness bears emerging from hibernation, typically seen along the coastlines looking for food.

Crowds and Prices: Fewer tourists imply a quieter experience, and cruise tickets are often lower. This is good for vacationers looking for a more calm journey and fantastic deals.

June: Milder Weather and Long Days

Weather and Scenery: June brings milder weather, with temperatures ranging from the 50s to 60s Fahrenheit. The days are longer, culminating in approximately 18 hours of daylight by the summer solstice. This prolonged daylight provides us more time to explore ports and enjoy stunning views.

Wildlife: June is the ideal time for whale watching since humpback and orca whales are commonly sighted. The fauna is rich, with many species active and visible.

Crowds and Prices: The season starts to build up, although it's not yet at its height. You may still locate relatively excellent discounts and enjoy moderate crowds.

July: Peak Season and Vibrant Activities

Weather and Scenery: July delivers the warmest weather, with temperatures frequently in the 60s and sometimes reaching the 70s Fahrenheit. The landscapes are lush and green, and the seas are often tranquil, giving it a perfect period for scenic cruises and outdoor activities.

animal: This is one of the greatest periods for animal viewing. Salmon runs draw bears to streams and rivers, and whales are still prevalent. You might also observe seals, sea lions, and a variety of birds.

Crowds and Prices: July is the peak of the cruise season, meaning higher prices and more people. It's the busiest time, so popular excursions could sell out quickly. Booking early is advisable.

August: Late Summer Splendor

Weather and Scenery: August continues the warm trend of July, with temperatures in the 50s to 60s Fahrenheit. The days start to shorten, but there's still plenty of daylight for activities. The scenery remains vivid and full of life.

Wildlife: Wildlife viewing continues outstanding, with ongoing opportunities to observe bears, whales, and other marine life. The salmon runs are in full flow, affording breathtaking vistas of nature in action.

Crowds and Prices: Crowds begin to thin gradually towards the end of the month, and prices may start to decline. It's a terrific opportunity to experience the peak season's perks with slightly fewer people.

September: Autumn Tranquility

Weather and Scenery: September brings milder temperatures, often in the 40s to 50s Fahrenheit. Fall colors begin to appear, creating a wonderful contrast to the green countryside. The days are shorter, but the sunsets can be magnificent.

Wildlife: This is a terrific time for viewing wildlife and preparing for winter. Bears are still active, and you might witness them fishing for the remainder of the salmon. Whale sightings are still possible, although they start to travel south.

Crowds and Prices: The season winds down in September, leading to fewer crowds and lower prices. It's a good time for people hoping for a calmer, more meditative encounter.

Overall Recommendations

Best for Wildlife: June and July offer the most constant and varied wildlife sightings.

Best for Budget Travelers: May and September give lower pricing and fewer crowds.

Best for Weather: July and August often offer the warmest and most steady weather.

The optimal time to sail to Alaska depends on your specific interests and priorities. Whether you're seeking seclusion and serenity, plentiful wildlife, or the ideal weather, there's a perfect moment for your Alaskan journey.

Choosing the Right Cruise Line and Ship

QSelecting the right cruise line and ship is a vital step in preparing your Alaska cruise vacation. The choice can substantially influence your overall experience, from the amenities accessible on board to the type of activities offered. Here's a detailed guide to help you make an informed decision:

Identifying Your Travel Preferences
Before looking into individual cruise lines and ships, evaluate your trip tastes and priorities:

Budget: Determine your budget, including the cost of the cruise, activities, and onboard charges.

Travel Style: Are you seeking luxury, adventure, family-friendly activities, or a more personal, small-ship experience?

Interests: Do you value animal viewing, cultural events, or outdoor activities like hiking and kayaking?

Duration: Decide how long you want your cruise to be, ranging from a week-long holiday to a two-week adventure.

Popular Cruise Lines for Alaska:
Overview of some of the top cruise lines that operate in Alaska, each catering to different categories of travelers:

Holland America Line

Best For Classic cruise experience, mature tourists, and those interested in cultural enrichment.

Highlights: Renowned for its vast Alaska itineraries, including Glacier Bay. Offers onboard programs with naturalists and historians.

Princess Cruises

Best For Families, first-time cruisers, and those wanting a blend of excitement and relaxation.

Highlights: Known for its "North to Alaska" program offering local cuisine, entertainment, and educational activities. Multiple ships with varying facilities.

Royal Caribbean

Best For Active travelers, families, and those searching for a large selection of onboard activities.

Highlights: Large ships with rock climbing walls, ice skating rinks, and other daring amenities. Diverse seaside trips.

Celebrity Cruises

Best For Couples, luxury seekers, and those wanting a modern, upscale experience.

Highlights: Offers opulent amenities, exquisite dining, and customized service. Focus on high-quality shore trips.

Norwegian Cruise Line

Best For Budget-conscious travelers, families, and those seeking flexible meal options.

Highlights: Freestyle cruise enables for varied dining times. Family-friendly activities and entertainment.

Regent Seven Seas Cruises

Best For Luxury travelers, couples, and those wanting an all-inclusive vacation.

Highlights: All-inclusive pricing covers excursions, great dining, and quality accommodations. Smaller ships for a more intimate experience.

UnCruise Adventures

Best For Adventure seekers, wildlife aficionados, and those wanting a small-ship experience.

Highlights: Focus on active and immersive experiences, including kayaking, hiking, and wildlife watching. Small ships that navigate into isolated locations.

Choosing the Right Ship:
Within each cruise company, ships differ in size, facilities, and onboard experiences. Here are some variables to consider:

Ship Size

Large Ships: Offer a wide choice of amenities such as several dining options, entertainment venues, and activities. Ideal for families and people who prefer a busy atmosphere.

Mid-Size Ships: Provide a balance of amenities and a more personal experience. Suitable for those who desire a combination of social activities and peaceful settings.

Small Ships: Can cruise into smaller ports and deliver a more customized experience. Perfect for adventure enthusiasts and those looking to discover off-the-beaten-path locales.

Onboard Amenities

Dining Options: Look for ships with numerous dining choices, including specialty restaurants and regional cuisine.

Entertainment and Activities: Consider what's essential to you, whether it's live entertainment, casinos, fitness centers, or enrichment programs.

Accommodation: Evaluate cabin alternatives, from budget-friendly interiors to opulent suites with private balconies.

Shore Excursions & Itineraries

Excursion Variety: Ensure the ship offers a selection of excursions that meet your interests, from cultural trips to adventure activities.

Port Stops: Check the schedule for must-see destinations and unique stops that correspond with your vacation goals.

Special Considerations:

Traveling with Kids: Look for family-friendly cruise lines like Disney Cruise Line or Royal Caribbean, which provide kids' clubs, family activities, and childcare services.

Accessibility: Ensure the ship is equipped with accessible rooms and facilities if you have mobility concerns.

Solo Travelers: Some cruise lines offer unique programs and accommodations for solo travelers, promoting a social environment.

Choosing the proper cruise line and ship is about aligning your preferences with the offerings of each option. Research thoroughly, read reviews, and consult with travel agencies if needed. Your Alaska cruise should be a remarkable excursion, and picking the correct cruise line and ship will set the stage for an amazing tour across the Last Frontier.

These are the contact details for the cruise lines mentioned:

Holland America Line

- **Website**: www.hollandamerica.com

- **Phone (U.S. & Canada):** 1-877-932-4259

- **Email**: Available through the contact form on their website

Princess Cruises

- **Website**: www.princess.com

- **Phone (U.S. & Canada):** 1-800-774-6237

- **Email**: Available through the contact form on their website

Royal Caribbean International

- **Website**: www.royalcaribbean.com

- **Phone (U.S. & Canada):** 1-866-562-7625

- **Email**: Available through the contact form on their website

Celebrity Cruises

- **Website:** www.celebritycruises.com

- **Phone (U.S. & Canada):** 1-888-751-7804

- **Email:** Available through the contact form on their website

Norwegian Cruise Line

- **Website:** www.ncl.com

- **Phone (U.S. & Canada):** 1-866-234-7350

- **Email:** Available through the contact form on their website

Regent Seven Seas Cruises

- **Website:** www.rssc.com

- **Phone (U.S. & Canada):** 1-844-473-4368

- **Email:** Available through the contact form on their website

UnCruise Adventures

- **Website:** www.uncruise.com

- **Phone (U.S. & Canada):** 1-888-862-8881

- **Email:** Available through the contact form on their website

Disney Cruise Line

- **Website:** [disneycruise.Disney.go.com](https://disneycruise.disney.go.com)

- **Phone (U.S. & Canada):** 1-800-951-3532

- **Email:** Available through the contact form on their website

For specific inquiries, it's frequently preferable to check the cruise line's website where you can find extensive contact information, including phone numbers for international clients and specialized departments.

Chapter 3. Cruise Itineraries

Common Routes and Ports of Call

Alaska cruises offer a range of itineraries that visit the state's magnificent scenery, abundant wildlife, and dynamic ports. While there are many possibilities to choose from, here are some of the most typical itineraries and ports of call you'll encounter:

Common Cruise Routes

Inside Passage

Description: The Inside Passage is a popular route that takes you across a network of picturesque waterways between the mainland and the islands of the Pacific Northwest. This route is recognized for its tranquil waterways, gorgeous scenery, and plentiful animals.

Highlights: Glacial fjords, lush woods, and lovely coastal towns.

Gulf of Alaska

Description: The Gulf of Alaska route normally entails a one-way trip between Vancouver or Seattle and Anchorage (Seward or Whittier). This route allows a more extended exploration of Alaska's shoreline.

Highlights: Opportunities to see more glaciers and a variety of ports on both the northern and southern ends of the tour.

Bering Sea and Beyond

Description: For those seeking a more adventurous and less-traveled route, some cruises venture into the Bering Sea, frequently involving stops in Russia's Far East and the Aleutian Islands.

Highlights: Remote and rough landscapes, diverse animals, and fewer crowds.

Highlights of Each Port

Juneau, the capital city of Alaska, is located between the high mountains of the Coast Range and the picturesque Gastineau Channel. Accessible only by boat or plane, it provides a unique blend of harsh wilderness and urban charm. The city is a gateway to the awe-inspiring Mendenhall Glacier, a huge river of ice that can be explored via hiking routes or up close on a guided trip. Adventure seekers can take the Mount Roberts Tramway, which ascends 1,800 feet for panoramic views of the city, mountains, and waterways below. Juneau's historic downtown district is packed with cultural attractions, including the Alaska State Museum and the lively waterfront dotted with stores, restaurants, and pubs offering fresh, local seafood. Whale-watching cruises and kayaking expeditions enable the opportunity to encounter abundant marine life, while the nearby forests and mountains offer limitless hiking and animal-viewing adventures.

Ketchikan, billed as the "Salmon Capital of the World," is a lively port perched on the edge of the Tongass National Forest. The community is noted for its rich Native Alaskan culture, apparent in the totem poles strewn across the area, especially those at the Totem Heritage Center and Saxman Totem Park. Visitors can explore the historic Creek Street, a boardwalk built on pilings spanning Ketchikan Creek, once the town's red-light district and now home to lovely stores and galleries. Ketchikan also serves as a gateway to the Misty Fjords National Monument, a spectacular wilderness area characterized by high cliffs, thick rainforests, and calm rivers excellent for exploring by boat or seaplane.

Skagway, a charming hamlet perched at the northern tip of Alaska's Inside Passage, is steeped in rich history from the Klondike Gold Rush era. Known for its well-preserved 19th-century houses and rustic wooden boardwalks, Skagway transports visitors back to a time of prospectors and pioneers. The town's historic area, part of the Klondike Gold Rush National Historical Park, provides museums, restored buildings, and vibrant reenactments.

A highlight for many visitors is the White Pass & Yukon Route Railroad, a picturesque train excursion that climbs approximately 3,000 feet to the peak of White Pass, affording stunning vistas of mountains, gorges, waterfalls, and ancient gold rush pathways. Outdoor enthusiasts can explore adjacent paths, such as the Chilkoot Trail, once traversed by optimistic gold miners.

Skagway's attractiveness extends to its vibrant local culture, with stores and cafés lining the streets, offering Alaskan goods and fresh seafood. The town's unique blend of natural beauty and historical significance makes it an intriguing destination on any Alaska cruise itinerary.

Sitka, set on Baranof Island in the Alexander Archipelago, is a lovely Alaskan town rich in history and natural beauty. With a unique blend of Russian and Tlingit heritage, Sitka offers a fascinating cultural experience. The magnificent St. Michael's Cathedral, a vestige of Russian colonial history, serves as a stunning landmark in the town center.

Surrounded by the gorgeous landscapes of the Tongass National Forest and facing the seas of Sitka Sound, the town gives numerous chances for outdoor excursions. Visitors can explore the Sitka National Historical Park, home to stunning totem poles and lush walking pathways. The Alaska Raptor Center offers a close-up look at rehabilitated birds of prey, including bald eagles.

Sitka's scenic harbor, thriving arts scene, and welcoming community make it a fascinating and enriching stop on any Alaska cruise itinerary.

Glacier Bay National Park is a pristine wilderness and a crown jewel of Alaska's natural treasures. Encompassing approximately 3.3 million acres, it boasts a beautiful scenery of towering glaciers, craggy mountains, temperate rainforests, and deep fjords. The park is famed for its tidewater glaciers, with Margerie and Johns Hopkins Glaciers being notable attractions. Visitors can experience the dramatic scene of calving, as enormous chunks of ice break off and crash into the water, causing deafening splashes.

Wildlife is abundant, with sightings of humpback whales, orcas, sea otters, and harbor seals often reported. On land, bears, moose, and mountain goats roam the various environments. Bird lovers will enjoy the variety of seabirds, including puffins and bald eagles.

The park is also deep in cultural history, home to the Huna Tlingit people, who have resided in the region for generations. Rangers often come aboard cruise ships to provide informative commentary, ensuring that passengers leave with a fuller appreciation of this wonderful natural reserve.

College Fjord, located on the northern side of Prince William Sound, is a beautiful glacial wonderland that offers an astounding mix of tidewater and valley glaciers. Named by a team of explorers from Harvard and Amherst in 1899, the fjord's glaciers retain the names of elite East Coast institutions, such as Harvard, Yale, and Vassar. The area is renowned for its calm beauty, with glaciers calving abruptly into the frigid waters below and flanked by steep, snow-capped mountains. Wildlife is abundant, with seals relaxing on ice floes and sea otters happily swimming in the fjord. The serene, chilly seas and the beautiful glaciers make College Fjord a highlight of any Alaska cruise, affording passengers breathtaking, panoramic vistas that are really unforgettable.

Hubbard Glacier is one of Alaska's most remarkable natural wonders, recognized for its huge size and dynamic nature. Stretching over 76 miles from its beginning in the Yukon Territory to its terminus at Disenchantment Bay, Hubbard is North America's largest tidewater glacier. The glacier's face towers about 400 feet above the waterline, with an additional 250 feet below the surface.

Visitors are typically awed by the glacier's vivid blue hues and the dramatic sounds of ice calving, where big chunks break off and fall into the bay, causing massive waves and loud roars. The surrounding scenery is equally stunning, with snow-capped peaks and clean lakes that reflect the glacier's majesty.

Accessible mostly by cruise ships and small expedition vessels, Hubbard Glacier offers a front-row seat to the raw, intense majesty of glacier action in one of the world's most remote and magnificent environments.

Victoria, the lovely capital of British Columbia, is recognized for its rich history, vibrant culture, and stunning coastline landscape. Nestled on Vancouver Island, this charming city features an assortment of Victorian-era architecture, reflecting its colonial background. Visitors can explore the famed Butchart Gardens, a floral wonderland with beautifully designed gardens and bright blooms year-round. The historic Inner Harbour is a lively hub, where you can enjoy waterfront cuisine, street entertainers, and views of the imposing British Columbia Parliament Buildings. The Royal BC Museum includes fascinating exhibitions on the region's natural and human history, making Victoria a blend of visual beauty and cultural depth.

Along the rugged coastline of Alaska's Inside Passage, Icy Strait Point offers a stunning blend of natural beauty, cultural legacy, and thrilling adventure. This secluded resort, near the Tlingit town of Hoonah, provides a unique opportunity to immerse oneself in the rich traditions of Alaska's indigenous peoples while surrounded by stunning surroundings.

As your cruise ship arrives at Icy Strait Point, you'll be welcomed by the sight of pristine woods, snow-capped mountains, and crystal-clear waterways filled with marine life. The ambiance is tranquil, with the air filled with the energizing aroma of pine and the soft sound of waves lapping against the shore.

Venturing ashore, you'll encounter a choice of activities that showcase the best of Alaska's wilderness. For those wanting excitement, opportunities abound, from zip-lining through the forest canopy to whale watching expeditions where you may observe spectacular humpback whales breaching the surface of the water.

Culture fans will find lots to explore as well. The neighboring Tlingit Heritage Center gives intriguing insights into the history, art, and traditions of the indigenous Tlingit people, with exhibitions showing elaborately carved totem poles, traditional regalia, and ancient artifacts.

Food enthusiasts won't be disappointed either, as Icy Strait Point provides a range of eating options serving up fresh, locally produced seafood and other Alaskan specialties. Whether you're seeking a substantial bowl of seafood chowder or ready to experience freshly caught salmon, there's something to satisfy every palate.

At the end of the day, when you wave farewell to Icy Strait Point and rejoin your cruise ship, you'll bring with you memories of a truly remarkable experience – a day spent discovering the untamed beauty and lively culture of one of Alaska's hidden treasures.

Petersburg, nicknamed "Little Norway," is a lovely village perched on the northern end of Mitkof Island in Southeast Alaska. Surrounded by spectacular coastline views and thick forests, Petersburg emits a fascinating blend of Scandinavian heritage and Alaskan wilderness.

Visitors to Petersburg are met by colorful Scandinavian-style buildings bordering the shoreline, affording a look into the town's rich cultural history. The community takes pride in its Norwegian roots, seen in the passionate celebrations of Norwegian festivals and the yearly Little Norway Festival.

Outdoor enthusiasts will find lots to explore in and around Petersburg. The area is recognized for its great fishing prospects, with salmon runs bringing fishermen from around the world. Visitors can also trek into the adjacent Tongass National Forest for hiking, animal viewing, and kayaking excursions.

For those interested in history and culture, Petersburg offers unique insights into its past. The Clausen Memorial Museum includes exhibits on the town's fishing economy, Norwegian heritage, and indigenous Tlingit culture. Visitors can also explore historic places like the Sons of Norway Hall and the Old Harbor Light.

Petersburg's inviting environment, magnificent surroundings, and rich cultural legacy make it a must-visit destination for those seeking an authentic Alaskan experience with a touch of Scandinavian flair.

Suggested Itineraries for Different Interests and Durations.

Wildlife & Nature Enthusiasts (7-Day Itinerary)

Day 1: Depart from Seattle or Vancouver, cruise through the Inside Passage.

Day 2: Explore Juneau, join a whale-watching excursion, or see Mendenhall Glacier.

Day 3: Cruise to Glacier Bay National Park, and enjoy the picturesque cruise and animal observation.

Day 4: Visit Skagway, and take a historic train trip on the White Pass & Yukon Route Railroad.

Day 5: Explore Ketchikan, visit the Tongass National Forest, or take a bear-watching tour.

Day 6: Scenic boating via Tracy Arm Fjord, observe beautiful glaciers and wildlife.

Day 7: Return to Seattle or Vancouver, and depart.

Adventure Seekers (10-Day Itinerary)

Day 1: Depart from Seattle or Vancouver, and cruise through the Inside Passage.

Day 2: Explore Victoria, British Columbia, and visit Butchart Gardens or kayak in the harbor.

Day 3: Cruise to Icy Strait Point, enjoy zip-lining, or take a whale viewing tour.

Day 4: Visit Sitka, go hiking in Tongass National Forest, or tour historic places.

Day 5: Cruise to Hubbard Glacier, enjoy a gorgeous cruise and picture possibilities.

Day 6: Explore Skagway, go on a glacier heli-hiking experience, or enjoy a kayak tour.

Day 7: Visit Juneau, try dog sledding on a glacier, or enjoy a magnificent flightseeing trip.

Day 8: Cruise through Glacier Bay National Park, and enjoy wildlife viewing and photography.

Day 9: Visit Ketchikan, try ziplining through the rainforest, or take a seaplane tour.

Day 10: Return to Seattle or Vancouver, and depart.

Cultural Explorers (14-Day Itinerary)

Day 1-3: Depart from Seattle or Vancouver, and cruise through the Inside Passage to Juneau.

Day 4: Explore Juneau, and visit the Alaska State Museum and Mendenhall Glacier.

Day 5: Cruise to Skagway, and experience the town's gold rush history and Klondike Gold Rush National Historical Park.

Day 6: Visit Haines, take a cultural tour of the Tlingit community, and experience traditional performances.

Day 7: Cruise to Glacier Bay National Park, and learn about Tlingit culture and history from onboard naturalists.

Day 8: Explore Sitka, and visit the Sitka National Historical Park and Russian Bishop's House.

Day 9: Cruise to Ketchikan, and explore Totem Bight State Historical Park and the Southeast Alaska Discovery Center.

Day 10-11: Visit Victoria, British Columbia, and see the Royal BC Museum and Craigdarroch Castle.

Day 12-14: Return to Seattle or Vancouver, depart.

These suggested itineraries offer a variety of activities customized to varied interests and lengths, allowing guests to customize their Alaska cruise adventure.

Chapter 3. What to Pack

Essential Items to Pack for an Alaska Cruise

Packing for an Alaska cruise demands careful preparation due to the region's unpredictable weather and the different activities you'll likely indulge in. Here's a list of important essentials to ensure you are prepared for a pleasant and pleasurable journey:

Clothing

Layers:

Base Layer: Moisture-wicking long-sleeve shirts and thermal tops.

Mid Layer: Insulating fleece or down coats.

Outer Layer: Waterproof and windproof jackets.

Pants:
Comfortable, quick-drying hiking pants.

Waterproof pants for excursions and rainy days.

Footwear:

Sturdy, waterproof hiking boots.

Comfortable walking shoes for shipboard and casual usage.

Accessories:

Warm hats and gloves for chilly weather.

Lightweight hat or cap for sun protection.

Scarf and neck gaiter for added warmth.

Gear and Accessories

Binoculars: For wildlife observation and beautiful cruising.

Camera: With extra batteries and memory cards to photograph spectacular scenery and wildlife.

Backpack: A modest daypack for excursions and coastal activities.

Waterproof Bag: To keep electronics and important items dry.

Reusable Water Bottle: To stay hydrated on excursions.

Sunglasses: With UV protection for sunny days and glacial glare.

Toiletries and Health

prescriptions: Any prescription prescriptions, plus seasickness cures and basic first aid supplies.

Sunscreen: Broad-spectrum SPF for protection against UV radiation.

Lip Balm: With SPF to protect against wind and sun.

Hand Sanitizer and Wipes: For cleanliness on excursions.

Documents and Essentials

Travel Documents:

- Passport or ID.
- Cruise tickets and itinerary.
- Shore trip vouchers and confirmations.

Money:

- Credit/debit cards.
- Some cash in tiny denominations for tips and local shopping.

Copies of Important Documents: Photocopies of your passport, insurance, and emergency contacts.

Comfort and Entertainment

Books and E-Readers: For leisure time onboard.

Chargers: For all electronic gadgets.

nibbles: Favorite nibbles for travels or downtime.

Travel Pillow and Blanket: For comfort during flights or long transfers.

Special Items

Swimsuit: For shipboard pools and hot tubs.

Formal Wear: For formal dining nights and special activities on the ship.

Insect Repellent: Especially if wanting to explore the forests and seaside areas.

Lightweight Gloves and Hat: For glacier visits and chilly days.

Pro Tips

Packing Cubes: To keep your luggage organized.

Laundry Bag: For soiled garments, making it easy to separate and handle.

Portable Power Bank: To keep gadgets charged during extended travels.

By bringing these essential goods, you'll be well-prepared for the different weather conditions and activities you'll encounter on your Alaska cruise, assuring a comfortable and memorable adventure.

General Weather Tips

Layering: The key to remaining comfortable in Alaska's variable weather is layering. Start with a moisture-wicking base layer, add an insulating mid-layer (such as fleece or down), and conclude with a waterproof and windproof outer layer. This method allows you to add or delete layers as needed.

Waterproof Clothing: Rain is typical in Alaska, regardless of the season. Waterproof coats, pants, and footwear are vital to staying dry and comfortable during excursions and on deck.

Footwear: Waterproof and robust hiking boots are essential for coastal excursions. Comfortable walking shoes are perfect for going onboard and exploring ports.

Accessories: Bring a warm hat, gloves, and scarf for cooler days, especially if you're visiting glaciers or higher elevations. Sunglasses and sunscreen are needed for sunny days and glacier glare.

Daylight Hours: Be prepared for lengthy daylight hours in June and July, which might disrupt sleep patterns. An eye mask might be beneficial. Conversely, expect shorter days as you reach the end of the season in September.

Temperature Variations: Even during the warmer months, mornings and evenings can be chilly. Always have an additional layer accessible for these times.

Onboard Weather Preparedness

Scenic Cruising: Decks can be windy and cool, even in summer. Dress in warm layers and bring a cap and gloves when spending time outside to thoroughly enjoy the environment.

Cabin Comfort: Most cabins are climate-controlled, however bringing comfy loungewear and a blanket can add extra comfort for lounging in your room.

Excursion Weather Considerations

Wildlife Viewing: Early mornings and late evenings can be cooler, but these are frequently the finest periods for wildlife sightings. Dress warmly and bring binoculars.
Adventure Activities: Activities like kayaking, hiking, and glacier trips may expose you to cold and damp weather. Ensure you have adequate gear and equipment for these trips.
Rain Gear: Even if the weather looks clear, carry a small, packable rain gear or poncho during shore excursions to be prepared for sudden showers.

By understanding Alaska's distinctive weather patterns and preparing accordingly, you can ensure a pleasant and enjoyable cruise experience, ready for whatever Mother Nature can offer.

Chapter 4. Onboard Experience

Accommodation Options

Suites on Alaska Cruises

Suites are the height of luxury and comfort on an Alaska cruise, offering spacious accommodations, increased amenities, and special services. These rooms often offer separate living and sleeping areas, big bathrooms with luxury furnishings, and private balconies with magnificent ocean views. Suites are suitable for people seeking greater space, privacy, and a higher degree of customized attention.

Features:

Space: Suites often range from 300 to over 1,000 square feet, providing adequate room to rest and unwind.

Living Areas: Separate living rooms with comfy seats, dining tables, and sometimes even a wet bar.

Bedrooms: Luxuriously equipped with high-quality bedding and ample storage space.

Bathrooms: Large bathrooms with bathtubs, walk-in showers, double vanities, and luxury amenities.

Balconies: Expansive private balconies with seats, excellent for admiring the stunning Alaskan scenery.

Facilities: Enhanced facilities include priority boarding and disembarkation, complimentary minibar, concierge service, and access to special lounges and dining spaces.

The cost of a suite on an Alaska cruise can vary greatly based on the cruise line, the exact ship, the time of year, and the kind of suite. On average, suite fares start around $2,500 to $4,000 per person for a 7-day cruise. More elegant or larger suites might vary from $5,000 to $10,000 or more per person.

Suites give an unrivaled cruising experience, combining elegance, comfort, and great service, making your Alaska voyage absolutely unforgettable.

Balcony Staterooms

Balcony staterooms are a popular accommodation choice on Alaska cruises, allowing visitors a private outside spot to view the stunning surroundings. These cabins often include floor-to-ceiling sliding glass doors that open onto a private balcony, providing a great area for sipping coffee while watching whales or appreciating the magnificent fjords and glaciers. The inside of a balcony stateroom normally features a nice bed, a sitting space with a sofa or chairs, a desk, and a private bathroom. Modern facilities like flat-screen TVs, mini-fridges, and Wi-Fi access are routinely available. The balcony itself is furnished with a small table and chairs, excellent for lounging and taking in the views.

The cost of a balcony stateroom on an Alaska cruise varies depending on the cruise line, the time of year, and the specific itinerary. On average, you should expect to pay between $1,500 and $3,500 per person for a 7-day trip. Prices may be higher during peak season (June to August), especially for luxury cruise lines or itineraries with more scenic cruising days. Booking in advance or looking for promotional packages can help secure a lower rate.

Oceanview Staterooms

Oceanview staterooms are a popular alternative for visitors who wish to experience the scenic grandeur of an Alaska cruise without the extra cost of a balcony berth. These accommodations feature a huge window or porthole that offers natural light and spectacular views of the ocean, mountains, glaciers, and wildlife as you sail. Oceanview cabins normally offer comfy mattresses, a private bathroom, adequate storage space, a lounge area, and conventional amenities such as a TV, mini-fridge, and safe. The window gives a constant link to the outside environment, making it easy to experience the ever-changing Alaskan landscape from the comfort of your room.

The cost of an oceanview cabin can vary substantially based on the cruise line, ship, time of year, and exact itinerary. On average, rates range from around $1,000 to $2,500 per person for a 7-day Alaska cruise. Early bookings, incentives, and last-minute offers can impact the ultimate pricing. For more deluxe or premium oceanview accommodations with additional facilities, the pricing may be greater. It's always wise to verify with the specific cruise line for the most updated pricing and availability.

Interior Staterooms

Interior staterooms are the most budget-friendly lodging option aboard a cruise ship. These cabins are located on the interior of the ship and do not have windows, which makes them perfect for travelers who favor price above views. Despite the absence of natural light, interior staterooms are often well-appointed with modern conveniences to ensure a comfortable stay.

Features:

44

Space: Generally compact, allowing efficient use of space with storage possibilities.

Amenities: Comfortable beds, a private bathroom with a shower, a TV, and often a small lounge space.

Location: Positioned in the middle of the ship, which can give a quieter environment and higher stability, lessening the impression of motion.

Interior staterooms are designed to be snug and pleasant, with beautiful decor and creative lighting techniques to create a friendly ambiance. While they may not have the benefit of natural lighting, they commonly incorporate mirrors and bright colors to improve the sensation of space and relaxation.

The cost of an inner stateroom on an Alaska cruise can vary greatly depending on the cruise line, the duration of the vacation, and the time of year. On average, you may expect to pay from $100 to $200 per person, per night. For a 7-night Alaska cruise, this corresponds to a total cost ranging from around $700 to $1,400 per person. Early bookings and last-minute discounts can occasionally give even reduced pricing.

Family Staterooms

Family cabins are built with the requirements of families in mind, offering extra space and handy facilities to ensure a pleasant and enjoyable cruise experience for all family members. These accommodations often have numerous sleeping places, such as bunk beds, pull-out sofas, or separate rooms to comfortably sleep several people. Additionally, family cabins frequently have extra storage space for goods, and some even have two bathrooms, making it easier for everyone to get ready for the day's activities.

The decor of family staterooms is frequently vibrant and inviting, appealing to both adults and children. Some cruise lines offer themed family staterooms with fun décor and kid-friendly features such as video game consoles or children's programs on the in-room entertainment system.

The cost of a family stateroom varies based on the cruise operator, ship, itinerary, and season. On average, you may expect to pay between $2,000 and $6,000 per week for a family of four. This pricing range might fluctuate greatly based on criteria such as cabin location, the amount of luxury, and the specific cruise line's services.

For example:

Budget Range: $2,000 - $3,000 (e.g., interior or basic oceanview family staterooms on popular cruise lines like Royal Caribbean or Carnival)

Mid-Range: $3,500 - $5,000 (e.g., balcony family staterooms on mid-tier cruise lines like Princess Cruises or Norwegian Cruise Line)

Luxury Range: $5,000 - $6,000+ (e.g., family suites or premium accommodations on luxury cruise lines like Disney Cruise Line or Celebrity Cruises)

Booking early and taking advantage of promos or discounts can also assist manage expenditures and obtain the finest stateroom for your family's needs.

The Haven (Norwegian Cruise Line)

The Haven is Norwegian Cruise Line's special enclave of exquisite cabins, allowing visitors a secluded and relaxing experience within the bigger ship. Located at the top of the ship, The Haven includes spacious rooms with upmarket amenities and individual service, creating a haven of calm and indulgence amidst the excitement of the journey.

Guests staying at The Haven enjoy a number of unique advantages, including priority embarkation and disembarkation, access to a private sundeck and pool area, and 24-hour butler service to tend to their every need. The suites themselves are attractively outfitted, with sophisticated décor, soft furnishings, and modern amenities such as flat-screen TVs, premium linen, and huge bathrooms with excellent bath products.

The Haven experience continues beyond the rooms, with specialized eating places reserved exclusively for Haven guests. These locations serve gourmet cuisine in an intimate setting, giving an upgraded culinary experience onboard.

The cost of staying in The Haven varies depending on criteria such as cruise route, suite category, and time of booking. Generally, accommodations in The Haven come at a premium compared to other staterooms on the ship, reflecting the higher degree of luxury and unique services. Prices typically start at several hundred dollars per person per night, with larger and more luxury suites commanding greater prices.

Dining and Cuisine

Fresh Alaskan King Crab
Fresh Alaskan King Crab is a culinary highlight of any Alaska cruise, famed for its sweet, delicious meat and remarkable size. Harvested from the frigid, pristine waters of the Bering Sea, these crabs are appreciated for their rich flavor and sensitive texture. Typically served steamed or boiled, the legs are commonly cracked open at the table, letting guests relish the juicy, savory meat. Enjoyed with drawn butter and a dash of lemon, this delicacy delivers a true flavor of Alaska's rich marine choices.

Wild-caught Alaskan Salmon is a gastronomic highlight on any Alaska cruise, praised for its rich flavor, solid texture, and high nutritional value. Harvested from the pristine seas of Alaska, this salmon is noted for its natural diet and sustainable fishing tactics, ensuring both quality and environmental responsibility. Guests can have it prepared in numerous ways, including as grilled, smoked, or poached, each manner accentuating its distinct, powerful taste. This delicacy is not only delicious but also filled with omega-3 fatty acids, making it a healthy choice for discriminating visitors.

Halibut is a treasured fish in Alaskan cuisine, recognized for its firm, white flesh, and mild, sweet flavor. It's a versatile fish that can be prepared in numerous ways, including grilling, baking, pan-searing, and even fish and chips. Halibut is typically featured in seafood dishes on Alaska cruises, appreciated for its delicate texture and rich taste. It's also a nutritional alternative, strong in protein and low in fat, making it a favorite among health-conscious tourists.

Enjoying fresh Alaskan halibut while cruising through the gorgeous surroundings adds to the true Alaskan experience.

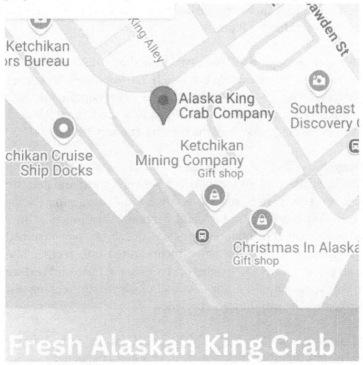

Scan the QR code
1. Open Camera: Launch your smartphone's camera app.
2. Position QR Code: Place the QR code within the camera's viewfinder.
3. Hold Steady: Keep the device steady for the camera to focus.
4. Wait for Scan: Wait for the code to be recognized.
5. Tap Notification: Follow the prompt to access the content.

Reindeer Sausage is a popular and unusual Alaskan delicacy, frequently loved by natives and visitors alike. Made from a combination of reindeer meat (typically blended with pig or beef for extra flavor and moisture), this sausage has a peculiar, slightly gamey taste. It is often seasoned with a blend of spices, including garlic, pepper, and coriander, giving it a deep and flavorful profile.

Reindeer sausage is often served grilled or pan-fried and can be relished in many dishes, such as hot dogs, breakfast platters, or on its own with mustard or other condiments. It's a must-try for anyone wishing to sample traditional Alaskan food, delivering a flavor of the region's culinary traditions.

Dungeness Crab is a popular and tasty seafood option on Alaska cruises, noted for its sweet, sensitive meat and delicate flavor. This variety of crab is often found along the Pacific Coast and is a culinary highlight for many vacationers. Often served steamed or boiling, Dungeness Crab can be consumed simply with melted butter or incorporated into recipes like crab cakes, salads, or spaghetti. Its unusual taste and texture make it a must-try for seafood enthusiasts seeking an authentic Alaskan dining experience.

Alaskan Black Cod (Sablefish), famed for its rich, buttery flavor and delicate, flaky texture, is a culinary delight on an Alaska cruise. This deep-sea fish, found in the chilly seas of the North Pacific, is commonly served using ways that showcase its natural taste, such as grilling, broiling, or smoking. It is generally served with minimum seasoning to let its innate flavor show, often complemented with fresh, local vegetables or a light sauce. Sablefish is not only delicious but also strong in omega-3 fatty acids, making it a healthy choice for seafood enthusiasts.

Clam Chowder on an Alaska cruise is a cozy and tasty dish, excellent for warming up on cooler days. This creamy soup is often cooked with fresh clams, soft potatoes, onions, and celery, and often adds a hint of smokiness from bacon. The rich, savory soup is thickened with cream or milk, resulting in a full and delicious dinner. Enjoying a bowl of clam chowder while taking in the gorgeous Alaskan surroundings makes a very unforgettable dining experience.

Baked Alaska is a classic dish that mixes contrasting textures and temperatures to produce a wonderful treat. It consists of a layer of sponge cake topped with ice cream, all wrapped in a thick layer of meringue. The entire dessert is then briefly baked in a very high oven until the meringue is golden and crisp, producing a striking contrast between the warm, fluffy surface and the cold, creamy ice cream interior.

On an Alaska cruise, Baked Alaska is sometimes served as a specialty dessert, highlighting the region's culinary traditions. Its dramatic look and excellent flavors make it a memorable finish to a gourmet meal, recalling the frigid landscapes of the Alaskan tundra.

Alaskan Cod Fish & Chips is a typical dish served on many Alaska cruises, delivering a taste of the region's bountiful fish. The dish typically comprises flaky Alaskan cod fillets wrapped in a crispy beer batter and served alongside golden-brown fries. Accompanied by tangy tartar sauce and a wedge of lemon, Alaskan Cod Fish & Chips is a pleasant and comforting dinner that accentuates the freshness and flavor of the local catch. It's a beloved choice for both lunch and dinner, delivering a hearty and excellent eating experience during your cruise over the gorgeous waters of Alaska.

Alaskan Amber Beer is a flagship brew of the Alaskan Brewing Company, situated in Juneau, Alaska. It's a traditional alt-style ale with a lengthy history stretching back to 1986 when it was originally made. This beer is noted for its balanced flavor profile, having a blend of malt sweetness and subtle hop bitterness. With a deep amber color and a smooth, clean finish, Alaskan Amber Beer is a popular option among beer fans and works well with a range of cuisines, making it a favorite onboard Alaska cruises for guests eager to savor a taste of the Last Frontier.

Entertainment and Activities

Live Music Performances onboard Alaska cruises provide visitors the opportunity to immerse themselves in a colorful and dynamic entertainment experience. Talented artists and bands present a varied spectrum of music genres, from jazz and blues to rock and pop, creating the perfect mood for relaxation and enjoyment. Whether it's calming acoustic melodies by the poolside, exciting performances in the ship's lounges and bars or fascinating plays in the main theater, live music adds an added layer of excitement and mood to the cruise journey. Guests can kick back, unwind, and appreciate the talent of the onboard musicians while appreciating the beautiful vistas of Alaska's breathtaking scenery.

Broadway-style Shows bring the thrill of musical theater to the high seas, offering guests a captivating entertainment experience. These plays feature professional performers, complex sets, stunning costumes, and live music, bringing iconic Broadway classics and innovative productions to life onboard cruise ships. From dazzling dance numbers to strong vocals, Broadway-style plays excite audiences with a blend of drama, comedy, and spectacle, making them a staple of the onboard entertainment roster. Whether it's a reinvented

Broadway hit or an original production produced particularly for the trip, these shows deliver an immersive and unique entertainment experience for guests of all ages.

Comedy Clubs onboard cruise ships provide guests an opportunity to unwind and enjoy laughter-filled nights with experienced comedians. These clubs often include a lineup of stand-up comedy acts, often with both family-friendly and adult-oriented shows to cater to varied audiences. The cozy and casual ambiance of the comedy club provides the perfect backdrop for visitors to enjoy a night of humor and entertainment, making it a popular choice for those wishing to add some fun to their cruise experience.

Movie Screenings provide passengers onboard Alaska cruises an opportunity to unwind and enjoy a cinematic experience while at sea. Typically staged in dedicated theaters or outdoor sites, these screenings present a variety of films ranging from recent blockbusters to vintage favorites. Whether it's a family-friendly animated movie, an exciting action thriller, or a romantic comedy, movie screenings provide entertainment for passengers of all ages and interests. It's a peaceful way to spend an evening or a quiet afternoon, replete with popcorn and comfortable chairs, bringing an added touch of delight to the cruise experience.

Dance Classes on an Alaska cruise offer a fun and interesting way to learn new dance forms or improve your skills while at sea. These sessions are often given by experienced instructors and include several genres, including ballroom, Latin, salsa, swing, and even line dancing. Suitable for all skill levels, dance sessions provide a fantastic opportunity to connect with fellow passengers, be active, and enjoy the music. Whether you're trying to grasp the basics or polish your technique, participation in dancing courses adds a dynamic and unforgettable experience to your cruise vacation.

Casino Games on an Alaska cruise provide passengers with a thrilling and sophisticated way to spend their evenings. Typically placed in an artistically built casino hall aboard the ship, these games include a variety of alternatives including slot machines, blackjack, poker, roulette, and craps. Whether you're a seasoned gambler or a newbie eager to try your luck, the cruise casino delivers an exciting and dynamic atmosphere with the potential to win big. Many ships also provide gaming classes and competitions, adding to the enjoyable and engaging experience of onboard entertainment.

Fitness Classes on an Alaska cruise provide travelers with a selection of options to stay active while enjoying spectacular views of the surrounding surroundings. These classes often include yoga, Pilates, Zumba, spin classes, and strength training sessions, all guided by trained teachers. Whether you're wanting to maintain your fitness regimen or try something new, the classes appeal to diverse skill levels and interests. They are frequently hosted in well-equipped fitness centers or on deck, providing a pleasant way to start or end your day amidst the spectacular Alaskan countryside.

Spa and Wellness Workshops

Spa and wellness seminars on an Alaska cruise provide passengers a chance to rest, refresh, and learn about holistic health methods in a tranquil setting. These courses are aimed to increase well-being through a variety of activities and therapies that cater to both physical and mental health.

Typical Offerings:

Yoga and Meditation Classes: Guided classes focused on mindfulness, stress reduction, and flexibility, often held on deck with spectacular ocean views.

Fitness sessions: From Pilates to high-intensity interval training (HIIT), these sessions cater to all fitness levels, helping guests stay active during their journey.

Nutrition & Wellness Seminars: Expert-led discussions on healthy eating, weight control, and nutritional suggestions to support a balanced lifestyle.

Spa Treatments: Indulge in a range of exquisite treatments, including massages, facials, body wraps, and aromatherapy sessions, all geared at promoting relaxation and renewal.

Beauty Workshops: Learn skincare routines, makeup skills, and hair care recommendations from pros, frequently showcasing luxury product lines.

Hydrotherapy Sessions: Experience the therapeutic benefits of saunas, steam rooms, and thalassotherapy pools meant to purify and stimulate the body.

Mindfulness & Stress Management: Workshops focused on techniques such as deep breathing exercises, guided imagery, and stress-relief routines to increase mental clarity and relaxation.

Detox Programs: Special programs that may include juice cleanses, herbal teas, and dietary recommendations to help cleanse and rejuvenate the body.

Benefits:

Holistic Well-being: Combining physical activity, mental relaxation, and dietary advice for a holistic wellness experience.

Personalized Attention: Many seminars offer personalized counsel and one-on-one sessions with wellness specialists.

Scenic Serenity: The serene backdrop of Alaska's natural beauty enhances the overall experience, making relaxation and awareness even more effective.

These seminars provide a perfect balance to the adventurous activities and excursions, ensuring that travelers come home feeling rested and invigorated.

Kids' Clubs and Activities

Alaska cruises are not just for adults; they provide a variety of kids' clubs and activities designed to keep younger travelers entertained and involved. These programs are often organized by age group to give age-appropriate entertainment, education, and fun. Here's a glance at what you may expect:

Age-Specific Clubs

Infants and Toddlers: Dedicated play spaces with age-appropriate toys, supervised playtime, and parent-and-child activities.

Kids (3-12 years): Split into several age groups, these clubs provide arts and crafts, science experiments, treasure hunts, themed parties, and interactive activities.

Teens (13-17 years): Teen lounges with video games, dance parties, sports tournaments, and social events aimed to help them make new friends and have fun in a safe atmosphere.

Adventure Ocean (Royal Caribbean)

Royal Caribbean's Adventure Ocean program is recognized for its extensive choice of activities, including scientific labs, themed parties, and outdoor expeditions. Kids can also enjoy scavenger hunts, talent showcases, and movie nights.

Disney Oceaneer Club and Lab (Disney Cruise Line)

Disney's dedicated kids' clubs offer beloved characters, immersive play areas, and interactive storytelling. The Oceaneer Club and Lab offer themed activities like Super Hero Training, Star Wars experiences, and craft projects inspired by Disney films.

Camp Discovery (Princess Cruises)

Partnered with Discovery™, Princess Cruises offers stimulating programs that include hands-on activities, science experiments, and wildlife encounters. The Treehouse, The Lodge, and The Beach House cater to different age groups with specialized experiences.

Splash Academy (Norwegian Cruise Line)

Norwegian's Splash Academy offers fun-filled activities such as circus school, arts & crafts, games, and team-building tasks. Teens have their own room called Entourage, with video games, movies, and dance parties.

Celebrity Cruises Camp at Sea

Celebrity Cruises offers a customizable program with over 500 activities, including STEM (Science, Technology, Engineering, and Mathematics) projects, culinary lessons, and arts and crafts. Teens have their own hangout space called The Basement.

Holland America Line Club HAL

Holland America Line's Club HAL includes a range of activities for youngsters and teens, including pirate treasure hunts, karaoke sessions, video game tournaments, and sports challenges.

Family Activities

Many cruise lines also provide family-oriented activities such as poolside games, family movie evenings, talent showcases, and shore excursions geared for all ages.

These kids' clubs and activities ensure that younger passengers have a great cruise experience, delivering a perfect blend of education, adventure, and entertainment, while giving parents some much-needed leisure time.

Chapter 5. Excursions and Activities

Popular Shore Excursions

Glacier Helicopter Tour

A Glacier Helicopter Tour delivers an amazing, bird's-eye view of Alaska's stunning glacial landscapes. Departing from numerous locations such as Juneau or Skagway, this adventurous tour begins with a breathtaking helicopter journey over rocky mountains, deep fjords, and expansive icefields. The chopper glides above enormous glaciers, affording amazing vistas of the frozen expanse below.

Passengers are rewarded with spectacular sights of towering ice spires, deep crevasses, and brilliant blue meltwater pools. The highlight of the excursion is landing straight on a glacier, where you may disembark and explore the bizarre, frozen scenery up close. Guided by professional pilots and glacier specialists, you'll learn about the development and movement of glaciers and the unique flora and wildlife that inhabit these icy habitats.

Walking on the glacier's surface, you'll feel the crunch of ancient ice beneath your boots and marvel at the clean, undisturbed splendor of this natural wonder. Photo opportunities abound, allowing you to capture the awe-inspiring panorama from this unique position.

The pricing for a Glacier Helicopter Tour normally runs from $300 to $450 per person, depending on the duration and exact elements of the tour.

Dog Sledding on a Glacier

Scan the QR code
1. Open Camera: Launch your smartphone's camera app.
2. Position QR Code: Place the QR code within the camera's viewfinder.
3. Hold Steady: Keep the device steady for the camera to focus.
4. Wait for Scan: Wait for the code to be recognized.
5. Tap Notification: Follow the prompt to access the content.

Dog sledding on a glacier is one of the most thrilling and iconic beach excursions available on an Alaska cruise. This journey often begins with a magnificent helicopter flight from

Juneau or Skagway, affording breathtaking aerial views of the harsh Alaskan scenery, towering mountains, and extensive icefields.

Upon landing on a gorgeous glacier, you are greeted by a team of excited sled dogs and their expert mushers. After a brief orientation, you jump into a traditional dog sled and go on an exciting adventure across the glacier's frozen expanse. The sensation of floating over the snow, pulled by a team of muscular huskies, is both thrilling and serene, with the only sounds being the rhythmic pattern of paws and the swoosh of the sled.

The experience generally includes time to interact with the dogs, learn about their training, and hear stories from the mushers about the history and culture of dog sledding in Alaska. The journey closes with another beautiful helicopter ride back, presenting a different viewpoint on the stunning surroundings below.

Mendenhall Glacier Ice Caves Exploration

The Mendenhall Glacier Ice Caves excursion is a really beautiful trip, allowing visitors a rare view into one of nature's most stunning wonders. Located just outside Juneau, Alaska, the Mendenhall Glacier is a vast river of ice, and its ice caves are a hidden gem beneath the glacier's surface.

Upon arrival, travelers begin on a guided journey through the harsh landscape of the Tongass National Forest, leading to the glacier's brink. The trek might be tough, needing strong boots and a good degree of fitness, but the reward is unsurpassed. Entering the ice caves, visitors are engulfed in a strange blue glow, with sunlight flowing through the ice, creating a stunning, otherworldly ambiance. The translucent ice walls, created over thousands of years, reveal a rainbow of blue hues and fascinating patterns, making for an amazing photo opportunity.

Inside the caves, the temperature lowers substantially, and the air is crisp and fresh. The sound of pouring water and the odd shatter of the ice contribute to the sensory experience, making it a genuinely immersive event. Expert guides assure safety while giving fascinating information about the glacier's genesis, history, and the environmental changes affecting it.

The Mendenhall Glacier Ice Caves exploration normally costs from $250 to $400 per person, depending on the tour operator and particular features like gear and transportation. Advanced booking is required owing to the demand and limited availability of these tours.

Prices for dog sledding on a glacier range from $500 to $600 per person, depending on the exact tour operator and duration of the expedition.

For additional information and booking, see

- [Alaska Shore Excursions](https://alaskashoreexcursions.com/juneau/dog-sledding-on-glacier-helicopter-tour).

ATV Adventures in Denali National Park

ATV Adventures in Denali National Park offers an amazing opportunity to experience the rough Alaskan wilderness. These guided tours take you off the usual path, allowing access to distant regions that are otherwise impossible to reach.

Riding through deep forests, across riverbeds, and along gorgeous ridgelines, you'll get the opportunity to observe spectacular scenery, from towering mountains to huge tundra.

Scan the QR code
1. Open Camera: Launch your smartphone's camera app.
2. Position QR Code: Place the QR code within the camera's viewfinder.
3. Hold Steady: Keep the device steady for the camera to focus.
4. Wait for Scan: Wait for the code to be recognized.
5. Tap Notification: Follow the prompt to access the content.

During the expedition, professional guides give information about the area's flora and animals, the park's geological features, and its rich history. You might spot wildlife such as moose, caribou, and bears in their native habitat. The ATV rides sometimes involve stops at stunning views, excellent for photography and soaking in the natural splendor.

Prices for ATV experiences in Denali National Park normally run from $125 to $200 per person, depending on the duration and exact tour package. Always check with the tour provider for the most current pricing and availability.

For booking, you can research possibilities on trustworthy tour websites such as [Denali ATV Adventures](https://www.denaliatv.com/).

Adventure Activities

Ice Climbing

Ice Climbing In Alaska is an exciting adventure that allows you to scale frozen waterfalls, glacial ice walls, and icy cliffs, delivering a unique and hard experience for adventure seekers. Guided by qualified instructors, climbers utilize specialized gear such as crampons, ice axes, and ropes to ascend the ice formations.

The climb normally starts with a safety briefing and basic instruction on ice climbing methods. As you proceed, you'll be mesmerized by the sheer grandeur of the freezing scene, with the glittering ice reflecting the pristine Alaskan wilderness. The experience combines physical endurance, technical expertise, and a feeling of adventure, rewarding climbers with stunning views and a profound sense of accomplishment.

Ice climbing expeditions sometimes take place in renowned sites such as Matanuska Glacier, where the towering ice cliffs create an exhilarating backdrop for this dangerous sport. Whether you're a seasoned climber or a beginner seeking a new challenge, ice climbing in Alaska guarantees an amazing trip in one of the world's most spectacular locations.

White Water Rafting

White water rafting in Alaska offers an adrenaline-pumping journey through some of the most spectacular and harsh environments in the world. As you traverse the roaring rapids of glacial-fed rivers, you'll be surrounded by towering mountains, deep woods, and plentiful animals.

Guided by trained pros, these rafting experiences cater to all ability levels, from beginner-friendly floats to demanding class IV rapids. You'll experience the exhilaration of crashing over waves, maneuvering around stones, and paddling through tumultuous waters. Along the route, you'll have the opportunity to spot species like eagles, bears, and moose, and to take in stunning views of glaciers and pristine environment.

Safety gear, including helmets and life jackets, is given, assuring a safe yet exhilarating experience. Whether you're seeking heart-pounding adrenaline or a peaceful river journey, white water rafting in Alaska is an unforgettable way to connect with nature and experience the state's natural splendor.

Glacier Hiking

Glacier Hiking is a thrilling and intimate experience, allowing you to see the stunning ice landscapes of Alaska up close. This journey entails traveling across glacial surfaces, negotiating through crevasses, and seeing ice creations that have been formed over millennia.

Equipped with crampons and supervised by trained personnel, trekkers travel the glacier's difficult terrain, feeling the crunch of ice beneath their feet. The climb affords breathtaking vistas of dazzling blue ice, towering seracs, and potentially even undiscovered ice caves. Along the route, guides give insights about the glacier's history, geology, and the environmental difficulties it faces.

Glacier hiking is not just a physical challenge but also a profound connection with one of nature's most powerful forces. It's a memorable journey that mixes physical exertion with awe-inspiring natural beauty, making it a must-do for thrill-seekers and nature fans.

Cultural Experiences: A Personal Journey

Exploring Alaska's rich cultural tapestry has been one of the most gratifying aspects of my cruise travels. The state's varied past, encompassing Native Alaskan traditions and historical influences from Russian pioneers, offers a unique and immersive experience.

On one unforgettable day in Ketchikan, I had the opportunity to visit the Totem Heritage Center. As I strolled around the museum, I marveled at the exquisite totem poles, each one presenting a distinct story of the Tlingit, Haida, and Tsimshian peoples. The sculptures showed animals and ancestral figures, each with significant symbolic implications. Listening to a local guide explain the meaning of the totems and the rituals underlying their production gave me a tremendous appreciation for this old art form.

Later, I participated in a traditional dance performance in Saxman Native Village. The rhythmic drumming and vivid costumes of the dancers were fascinating. I felt honored to observe the community's attempts to preserve its cultural legacy and share it with outsiders like me. The stories portrayed through their dances were both strong and emotional, allowing an insight into their rich spiritual world.

In Sitka, I visited the Sitka National Historical Park, where I wandered along trails adorned with totem poles and historical sites. The highlight was a visit to the Russian Bishop's House, a reminder of Alaska's Russian colonial past. The contrast between Native Alaskan and Russian influences was interesting, providing a deeper appreciation of the region's complex past. One of the most intimate cultural encounters was a visit to a Tlingit clan residence in Hoonah. Sitting in the warmth of the communal house, I listened to elders recounting legends and stories passed down through centuries. The sense of togetherness and the importance of storytelling in preserving their culture were obvious. I even got to eat traditional meals like smoked salmon and frybread, connecting with the local cuisine.

These cultural experiences have tremendously enhanced my perspective of Alaska. They've helped me to connect with the state on a deeper level, beyond its natural beauty and fauna. Through these meetings, I've gotten a greater appreciation for the tenacity and vibrancy of Alaska's native cultures and the numerous influences that have created its past. It's an aspect of my travels that I cherish and look forward to exploring further on future visits.

Chapter 6. Wildlife and Nature

Key Wildlife to Look For

Bald Eagles:
Bald eagles, the majestic icons of American freedom, are a sight to behold in Alaska. These gorgeous birds, with their distinctive white heads and tails, contrasted against dark brown bodies, can often be seen soaring effortlessly above the rough coastline and towering woodlands. With wingspans reaching up to 7 feet, they command the skies with an awe-inspiring presence.

During my Alaska trip, witnessing bald eagles perched high on tree branches or swooping over the lake was a delight. Their acute eyesight allows them to see fish from vast heights, and watching them descend with tremendous speed and precision to seize their prey from the water's surface was an exciting experience. Observing these formidable raptors in their native home, amidst the stunning Alaskan wilderness, underlined the region's great biodiversity and the crucial role bald eagles play in its ecosystem.

Humpback Whales are beautiful oceanic mammals noted for their awe-inspiring size, acrobatic displays, and mournful songs. These gentle giants can reach lengths of up to 60 feet and weigh as much as 40 tons, making them one of the largest mammals on the planet.

Found in oceans around the world, humpback whales are famous for their annual migrations, during which they travel hundreds of kilometers between feeding and mating locations.

Alaska's coastal seas, particularly the Inside Passage and Glacier Bay, are great sites for encountering these spectacular creatures throughout the summer months.

One of the most captivating qualities about humpback whales is their behavior. They are famed for their dramatic breaching, as they thrust themselves out of the water and crash back down with a thunderous splash. They also display additional behaviors such as tail slapping, flipper waving, and bubble net feeding, where they work together to corral and capture fish.

Beyond their physical prowess, humpback whales are also famed for their intricate vocalizations, commonly referred to as "singing." These mournful songs, which may linger for hours, are thought to have a part in mating rituals and communication among individuals.

Encountering humpback whales in the wild is a genuinely magical experience, allowing an insight into the life of these intelligent and intriguing creatures. Whether observed from the deck of a cruise ship or up close on a whale-watching expedition, the sight of these majestic animals is guaranteed to leave a lasting effect on anybody lucky enough to see them.

Orcas, commonly known as Killer Whales, are one of the most iconic and spectacular marine species found in the waters of Alaska. These very clever and gregarious creatures attract with their sleek black and white bodies and unique dorsal fins.

Orcas are apex predators, recognized for their extraordinary hunting abilities and intricate social structures. They hunt in pods, often working together to pursue their prey, which can include fish, seals, and even other whales. Witnessing an orca pod in action is a fascinating sight, as they breach, spy-hop, and slap their tails in demonstrations of force and agility.

Orcas are also noted for their vocalizations. They communicate using a sophisticated system of clicks, whistles, and calls, which play a significant role in their social relationships and navigation.

Encountering orcas in the wild is a truly awe-inspiring event. Whether observing them from the deck of a cruise ship or attending a specialist whale-watching expedition, witnessing these majestic creatures in their natural habitat leaves a lasting effect on those who have the chance to see them.

Grizzly Bears are renowned emblems of the Alaskan environment, recognized for their enormous size, power, and fearsome presence. These wonderful species can be found across the state, particularly in coastal areas, woods, and hilly regions.

With their unique humped shoulders and powerful frame, grizzly bears are well-adapted to live in Alaska's rough terrain. They are omnivores, grazing on a wide diet that includes fish, berries, roots, and small mammals. During the summer months, grizzlies can often be spotted fishing for salmon in rivers and streams, exhibiting their remarkable hunting skills.

Encountering a grizzly bear in the wild is an exciting and awe-inspiring experience, but it's necessary to view them from a safe distance and with respect for their habitat. These apex predators serve a key role in maintaining the balance of ecosystems and are an integral element of Alaska's natural history.

Seeing a grizzly bear in its native habitat is a reminder of the raw beauty and untamed wildness that distinguishes Alaska, making it a highlight of any wildlife enthusiast's journey.

Black Bears

Black bears are one of the most iconic and regularly spotted creatures in Alaska, recognized for their unique behavior and adaptability. These lovely creatures, with their glossy black coats, can often be spotted foraging in the woodlands and along the riverbanks. Weighing between 150 and 600 pounds, black bears are omnivores, devouring a wide diet that includes berries, fish, nuts, and plants.

During my Alaskan trip, I got the thrilling opportunity to watch a black bear in its natural habitat. Standing silently on a guided tour in the Tongass National Forest, I watched as the bear successfully fished for salmon in a raging stream. Its muscular paws and keen sense of smell made it an adept hunter, and seeing it up close was both humbling and awe-inspiring.

Black bears are mainly solitary animals, save during mating season or when a mother is caring for her offspring. Their presence in the wild is a reminder of the remarkable biodiversity that survives in Alaska's pristine settings. Observing these animals in the wild provides a greater connection to the natural world and a profound awareness of the delicate balance of the ecosystem they inhabit.

Best Times and Places for Wildlife Viewing

Alaska is a wildlife enthusiast's heaven, offering many opportunities to observe its unique animals. Knowing the ideal times and places to watch animals can enhance your experience substantially. Here's a strategy to maximize your chances of spotting some of Alaska's most recognizable animals:

Best Times for Wildlife Viewing

Spring (April to June):

Bird Migration: Spring sees the arrival of millions of migrating birds, including Arctic terns and puffins. Coastal locations and bird sanctuaries are great spots.

Marine Mammals: This season sees gray whales migrate northward, and humpback whales return to feeding sites.

Moose Calving: Early spring is the ideal time to witness newborn moose calves.

Summer (June to August):

Peak Wildlife Activity: Long daylight hours and higher temperatures mean animals are more active and noticeable. Bears, especially, are regularly spotted fishing for salmon in rivers.

Whale Watching: Humpback whales are prevalent in places like Glacier Bay and the Inside Passage.

Caribou Migration: Herds can be spotted in the Arctic regions and Denali National Park.

Fall (September to October):

Bear Viewing: Bears are still busily feasting on salmon in preparation for hibernation. Katmai National Park is noted for its bear population.

Salmon Runs: Late summer to early fall is the greatest time to observe large salmon runs, which attract bears and eagles.

Winter (November to March):

Northern Lights: While not wildlife, the Aurora Borealis is a beautiful natural phenomenon best witnessed over the long winter nights.

Moose and Caribou: These species are easy to identify against the snowy backdrop, especially in locations like Anchorage and Fairbanks.

Best Places for Wildlife Viewing

Denali National Park:

Home to the "Big Five" (grizzly bears, wolves, moose, caribou, and Dall sheep).

Prime animal viewing on Denali Park Road.

Kenai Fjords National Park:

Rich in marine life, including orcas, humpback whales, sea otters, and puffins.

Offers spectacular glacier and coastal views.

Katmai National Park:

Famous for brown bear watching, notably near Brooks Falls where bears fish for salmon.

Glacier Bay National Park:

Ideal for whale watching and spotting seals, sea lions, and bald eagles.

Scenic beauty with glaciers and fjords as a backdrop.

Kodiak Island:

Known for its big population of Kodiak bears.
It also offers superb bird watching and maritime fauna.

Wrangell-St. Elias National Park:

The largest national park in the U.S., home to a broad range of species including bears, moose, and mountain goats.

Prince William Sound:

Renowned for sea kayaking and watching marine species like orcas, humpback whales, and sea otters.

Chilkat Bald Eagle Preserve:

Located near Haines, this area attracts the world's biggest concentration of bald eagles, especially in late fall.

Anan Wildlife Observatory:

Situated near Wrangell, it's one of the best spots to view black and brown bears fishing for salmon.

Sitka:
Offers diverse marine life, including sea otters, whales, and seals, along with lovely coastal views.

By planning your vacation around these prime times and areas, you'll considerably boost your chances of experiencing

Alaska's amazing wildlife in their native environments. Whether it's the thrill of spotting a grizzly bear or the awe of watching a whale breach, Alaska delivers unique wildlife encounters.

Natural Landmarks and Scenic Highlights

Lake Clark National Park.

Lake Clark National Park is one of Alaska's most spectacular and inaccessible natural gems. Located in the southern portion of the state, this huge park comprises over four million acres of pure wilderness, providing visitors with a spectacular mix of scenery, from steep mountains and glacial lakes to lush woods and expansive tundra.

The focus of the park is the beautiful Lake Clark, a huge, turquoise lake encircled by towering peaks and active volcanoes. The lake's crystal-clear waters mirror the spectacular surroundings, providing a fascinating spectacle that captivates those who visit. The park's namesake lake is not only picturesque but also a hub for several leisure activities, including kayaking, fishing, and boating.

Exploring the park, travelers discover beautiful volcanoes like Mount Redoubt and Mount Iliamna, which dominate the skyline. These snow-capped giants provide a feeling of majesty and adventure to the area. The park's different ecosystems sustain a great diversity of species, making it a haven for nature enthusiasts and photographers. Bears are regularly sighted fishing for salmon in the park's rivers, while moose, caribou, and wolves wander the wilderness.

For those seeking isolation and a connection with nature, Lake Clark National Park offers unequaled options for backcountry hiking and camping. Trails travel through lush forests, across alpine meadows, and up to high summits with panoramic views of the surrounding wilderness. The park's seclusion means visitors can typically see its natural beauty without the crowds experienced in more accessible places.

Lake Clark National Park and Preserve

Scan the QR code

1. Open Camera: Launch your smartphone's camera app.
2. Position QR Code: Place the QR code within the camera's viewfinder.
3. Hold Steady: Keep the device steady for the camera to focus.
4. Wait for Scan: Wait for the code to be recognized.
5. Tap Notification: Follow the prompt to access the content.

One of the unique qualities of Lake Clark is its cultural legacy. The area has been inhabited by Indigenous peoples for thousands of years, and their presence is still felt today. Visitors can learn about the Dena'ina Athabascan culture and history through interpretive programs and by visiting historical sites inside the park.

Whether you're an adventurer looking to explore tough terrain, a wildlife enthusiast eager to witness creatures in their natural habitat, or a traveler seeking the calm and beauty of Alaska's undisturbed wilderness, Lake Clark National Park offers an amazing experience. Its spectacular vistas, plentiful animals, and tranquil seas make it a must-visit location for anybody visiting the natural wonders of Alaska.

Chugach State Park

Chugach State Park, located just outside Anchorage, is one of the largest state parks in the United States, spanning nearly 500,000 acres. This enormous wilderness offers a spectacular diversity of scenery, including rough mountains, lush woods, alpine tundra, and glacier lakes.

Visitors to Chugach State Park can enjoy a choice of outdoor activities. Hiking paths range from short treks to strenuous climbs, with popular routes like Flattop Mountain affording panoramic views of Anchorage and the surrounding surroundings. Wildlife is abundant, and it's common to observe moose, black bears, and Dall sheep. The park's rivers and streams give good chances for fishing, notably for salmon and trout.

In winter, Chugach changes into a mecca for snow sports aficionados, with possibilities for cross-country skiing, snowshoeing, and even ice climbing. The park's stunning splendor and proximity to Anchorage make it a year-round destination for both locals and visitors seeking to experience the pristine Alaskan wilderness.

Gates of the Arctic National Park

Gates of the Arctic National Park, located in northern Alaska, is a huge and remote wilderness area that symbolizes unadulterated natural splendor. Covering over 8 million acres, it is the second-largest national park in the United States and one of the least visited, allowing a true escape into the wild.

The park is named for two spectacular peaks, Frigid Crags and Boreal Mountain, which frame the Koyukuk River, forming a natural "gate" into the Arctic. The terrain is distinguished by rocky mountains, wide tundra, glacially carved valleys, and pure rivers. It's home to rich wildlife, including caribou, grizzly bears, wolves, Dall sheep, and various bird species.

Visitors to Gates of the Arctic must be self-sufficient, as there are no roads, trails, or visitor services within the area. Access is mainly by bush aircraft, and activities include backpacking, hiking, camping, and float trips along the park's untamed rivers. The absence of modern services and infrastructure provides for a pure and immersive experience in one of the few true wilderness locations on Earth.

The park also retains cultural value, with Native Alaskan groups such as the Iñupiat and Athabascan peoples having lived in harmony with the land for thousands of years. Gates of the Arctic National Park offers an unprecedented opportunity to witness the raw, majestic majesty of the Arctic terrain and to understand the fragile balance of its ecology.

Mount Redoubt.

Mount Redoubt is a remarkably spectacular stratovolcano found in the Aleutian Range of Alaska. Standing at 10,197 feet, it's one of the most prominent peaks in the region and part of the Ring of Fire, famed for its volcanic activity. The volcano's snow-capped peaks and craggy slopes make a magnificent contrast against the sky.

Visible from the Kenai Peninsula, Mount Redoubt has a historic history of eruptions, with noteworthy activity in 1989-1990 and 2009. These eruptions have drastically changed the landscape, blasting ash clouds high into the atmosphere and causing broad lava flows.

For anyone lucky enough to witness it, either from an aircraft or on a clear day from the ground, Mount Redoubt offers an awe-inspiring peek into the dynamic geological forces at play in Alaska. Its tremendous presence and the surrounding wilderness underscore the raw beauty and unpredictability of the natural world.

Hubbard Glacier

Hubbard Glacier, located in eastern Alaska and part of Yukon, Canada, is one of the most stunning natural monuments in the region. Spanning over 76 miles in length and reaching up to 600 feet above the ocean, it is the longest tidewater glacier in North America. This huge glacier is famed for its magnificent blue ice, which originates from the compression of snow, expelling air bubbles and allowing light to penetrate deeply.

Visiting Hubbard Glacier is an awe-inspiring experience. As you approach by cruise ship or tour boat, the sheer scale of the glacier becomes clear. The front face of the glacier, known as the terminus, is an active area where ice frequently calves, sending enormous chunks cascading into the bay with deafening splashes. These enormous icefalls create small tsunamis and provide a breathtaking demonstration of nature's raw strength.

The surrounding beauty adds to the glacier's attractiveness, with snow-capped mountains and pure waters making a stunning backdrop. Wildlife observations are plentiful in the region, with seals often lazing on ice floes and seabirds swooping overhead. The bright blue hues of the ice, the crisp air, and the sound of breaking ice make a visit to Hubbard Glacier a sensory feast, leaving visitors with unforgettable memories of this beautiful natural wonder.

Chapter 7. Tips for a Smooth Trip

Navigating the Cruise Terminal

Navigating the cruise terminal can be an exciting start to your Alaska cruise vacation. Here's a guide to assist you in smoothly navigating the terminal and embarking on your journey:

Arrival and Check-In:

Upon arrival at the terminal, follow signs or directions from port workers to the check-in area.

Have your travel documentation, including passport, cruise ticket, and any required health forms, conveniently accessible for check-in.

Baggage Drop-off:

If you have checked your luggage, continue to the baggage drop-off area where porters will assist you.

Ensure your luggage tags are securely affixed to your bags with your cabin number plainly visible.

Security Screening:

Pass through security screening, similar to airport processes, where your carry-on baggage will be scanned.

Be prepared to remove metal objects, electronics, and liquids from your bags.

Check-In Process:

Approach the check-in counter where you'll produce your travel documents and receive your cruise ID card.

This card acts as your identification and onboard payment mechanism, so keep it safe throughout your vacation.

Boarding Process:

Once checking in, head to the boarding area and await directions from port workers.

Boarding normally occurs in groups or by scheduled embarkation times, so listen for announcements or follow signage.

Security and Customs:

Pass through security and customs clearance before boarding the ship.

Have your cruise ID card and travel paperwork available for inspection.

Onboard Welcome:

Upon boarding, you'll be greeted by the ship crew who will show you to your accommodation and deliver crucial information regarding onboard facilities and safety protocols.

Take some time to explore the ship and familiarize yourself with its layout before departure.

Enjoy Your Cruise:

Once settled into your stateroom, relax and enjoy the start of your Alaska cruise trip!

Take advantage of onboard activities, eating options, and stunning vistas as you set sail for your destination.

Health and Safety Tips for Your Alaska Cruise

Ensuring your health and safety throughout your Alaska cruise is crucial for a worry-free and pleasurable vacation. Here are some recommendations to help you stay safe and healthy throughout your journey:

Pack Essentials:

Bring vital prescriptions and a first-aid kit tailored to your needs.

Include goods like pain relievers, motion sickness medication, sunscreen, bug repellent, and hand sanitizer.

Stay Hydrated:

Drink plenty of water, especially in Alaska's chilly environment, to stay hydrated and prevent dehydration.

Practice Good Hygiene:

Wash your hands frequently with soap and water for at least 20 seconds, especially before eating and after using the restroom.

Use hand sanitizer with at least 60% alcohol if soap and water are not available.

Follow COVID-19 Protocols:

Adhere to the cruise line and port authority rules for COVID-19 safety protocols, including mask-wearing, social distancing, and testing requirements.

Stay informed about any updates or changes to COVID-19 policies both before and during your voyage.

Be Sun Smart:

Apply sunscreen with a high SPF often, especially if you'll be spending time outdoors on deck or during shore excursions.

Wear protective clothing, sunglasses, and a wide-brimmed hat to shelter yourself from the sun's dangerous UV rays.

Practice Safe Dining:

Follow food safety recommendations and avoid consuming undercooked or raw foods, especially shellfish.

Wash fruits and vegetables thoroughly before eating.

Stay Active:

Take advantage of onboard workout facilities and participate in outdoor activities like walking, hiking, or cycling during port calls to keep active and maintain general well-being.

Be Prepared for Emergencies:

Familiarize yourself with the ship's emergency protocols, including evacuation routes and assembly stations.

Know how to contact ship personnel or medical staff in case of an emergency.

Stay Informed:

Stay knowledgeable on weather conditions, wildlife safety, and any potential threats in the areas you'll be visiting.

Listen to aboard announcements and heed any safety warnings from ship officials.

Respect Wildlife:

Maintain a safe distance from wildlife during shore excursions and obey park guidelines to avoid disturbing or endangering animals.

By following these health and safety precautions, you can enjoy a safe and fulfilling Alaska cruise trip, packed with wonderful moments and stunning adventures. Remember to prioritize your well-being and take necessary safeguards to guarantee an enjoyable and worry-free experience.

Budgeting and Saving Money

Planning and budgeting for your Alaska cruise will help you get the most out of your holiday without overspending. Here are some ways to help you manage your cash effectively:

Set a Realistic Budget:

Determine your overall budget for the cruise, including transportation, lodging, onboard expenses, and shore excursions.

Break down your budget into categories to allocate funds correctly.

Book Early for Discounts:

Take advantage of early booking discounts and specials given by cruise lines.

Booking in advance might also provide more alternatives for cabin selection and preferred travel dates.

Consider Off-Peak Travel Times:

Traveling during shoulder seasons or off-peak times can typically result in lower cruise fares and reduced travel expenditures.

Research the best times to visit Alaska to locate the most economical options.

Compare Prices:

Compare costs from different cruise lines and travel companies to discover the best offers.

Look for package offers that may include airfare, hotel accommodations, or onboard credits.

Look for Special Offers:

Keep an eye out for special offers, promotions, and discounts offered by cruise companies, especially for last-minute bookings.

Subscribe to newsletters or follow cruise lines on social media to remain updated about exceptional bargains.

Opt for Value-Added Packages:

Consider purchasing value-added packages for services like meals, beverages, or shore excursions.

These packages may offer savings compared to purchasing products individually onboard.

Limit Onboard Expenses:

Set a daily spending limit for onboard expenses such as drinks, souvenirs, and spa treatments.

Take advantage of complimentary onboard activities and amenities to save money.

Pack Wisely:

Pack basic goods like sunscreen, prescriptions, and toiletries to avoid purchasing them onboard at inflated prices.

Bring reusable water bottles to refill onboard instead of purchasing bottled water.

Plan Shore Excursions Wisely:

Research and book shore excursions independently to potentially save money compared to booking through the cruise line.

Consider other options like self-guided excursions or exploring ports on your own to economize on excursion charges.

Track Your Spending:

Keep track of your expenses throughout the vacation to avoid overpaying.

Monitor your onboard account often to ensure it corresponds with your budget and to spot any inconsistencies early.

Set Aside Emergency Funds:

Plan for unforeseen expenses or crises by setting aside a percentage of your budget as a contingency reserve.

Having additional finances accessible can bring peace of mind and help cover unforeseen bills.

Chapter 8. Resources And Itineraries

Example Daily Schedule for a 7–10 Day Cruise

Use this sample 7–10-day cruise itinerary to embark on an amazing tour through Alaska's breathtaking landscapes and varied wildlife:

Day 1: Leaving Seattle, Washington
In Seattle, Washington, board your cruise ship and get comfy in your cabin.

Explore the ship's facilities, including dining options, lounges, and entertainment areas, and attend a welcome orientation.

Set sail for your Alaskan adventure and leave the busy metropolis behind.

Day 2: Out at Sea Sail for your first point of call and enjoy a full day at sea. Benefit from the facilities and activities offered on board, such as spa services, fitness courses, and informative talks on Alaska's animals and culture. Savor delectable food, unwind by the pool, and take in the expansive views of the Pacific Ocean.

Day 3: Juneau, Alaska: Get to Juneau, the state capital of Alaska, which is surrounded by unspoiled wilderness and tall mountains.

Visit the Alaska State Capitol, stroll around the historic downtown district, and browse local boutiques for trinkets.

Take part in extra shore excursions including a helicopter flight to the Juneau Icefield, whale watching, or glacier trekking.

Day 4: Skagway, Alaska-Dock in Skagway, a little town with a rich Gold Rush past and stunning surroundings.

Take a trip on the historic White Pass & Yukon Route Railroad or visit the Klondike Gold Rush National Historical Park to travel back in time. Hike, kayak, or explore the untamed landscape of the neighboring Tongass National Forest while you go on outdoor excursions.

Day 5: Glacier Bay National Park: Take a cruise through the UNESCO-designated Glacier Bay National Park, which is known for its breathtaking animals and glaciers. Admire the imposing ice walls, hear the roaring calving of glaciers, and watch for animals like bald eagles, sea otters, and humpback whales. Throughout the day, park rangers on board offer insightful commentary on the environmental and cultural history of the park.

Day 6: Alaska's Ketchikan Get to Ketchikan, the "Salmon Capital of the World" with a thriving Native American community. Take a wilderness excursion in the Tongass National Forest, tour historic Creek Street, or stop by the Totem Heritage Center. Optional activities include a magnificent flightseeing tour over Misty Fjords National Monument, zip-lining through the jungle, and salmon fishing.

Day 7: British Columbia's Victoria (Optional) Visit Victoria, British Columbia, which is renowned for its historic buildings, quaint gardens, and British influence. Explore the historic Inner Harbor, have high tea at the Fairmont Empress Hotel, or visit the famous Butchart Gardens. Before heading back to the ship, take a stroll through the city's charming streets in the evening.

Day 8: you return to Seattle, where you depart from your cruise ship and say goodbye to your fellow passengers.

Stay longer in Seattle to take in the sights, such as the Museum of Pop Culture, Pike Place Market, and the Space Needle.

Day 9–10: Optional Post-Cruise Extension: To further explore Seattle or other neighboring locations like Olympic National Park or the San Juan Islands, think about adding a post-cruise extension to your stay.

On this 7–10 day cruise itinerary, which is full of amazing adventures, stunning scenery, and engaging cultural experiences, discover the wonder and beauty of Alaska.

Tour operators' contact details

Shore Tours of Alaska:

- [www.alaskashoretours.com] is the website. The website https://alaskashoretours.com/

- **Contact information**: info@alaskashoretours.com; phone: 1-888-586-8489

The Tour Operator:

- [www.thetourcompany.com/alaska] is the website.(https://www.thetourcompany.com/alaska) - Contact: info@thetourcompany.com - Telephone: 1-800-555-1234

Alaska's Wilderness Adventures:

- [www.wildernessadventuresalaska.com] is the website. The website https://www.wildernessadventuresalaska.com/ also

- **Contact information**: info@wildernessadventuresalaska.com; phone: 1-907-123-4567

Alaska Excursions:

- [www.alaskaexcursions.com] is their website.The website https://www.alaskaexcursions.com/

- **Contact information**: info@alaskaexcursions.com; phone: 1-800-123-7890

Tours of the Northern Lights:

- [www.northernlightstoursalaska.com] is the website.(Northernlightstoursalaska.com/)

- Contact information: info@northernlightstoursalaska.com; phone: 1-907-555-6789

To improve your Alaska cruise experience, these tour companies provide a range of excursions and activities. For more details, availability, and booking information, get in touch with them directly.

Bonus: Advice on Photography

One of the best ways to preserve memories of the amazing scenery, wildlife encounters, and cultural experiences during your Alaska cruise is to take beautiful pictures. Here are some photography techniques to help you capture Alaska's beauty with a digital camera or smartphone:

Be Aware of Your Equipment: Before your vacation, become familiar with the functions and settings of your digital camera or smartphone. Discover how to change parameters including white balance, focus, and exposure.

Packing necessary accessories: Don't forget to pack spare batteries, memory cards, lens cleaning cloths, and a case for your smartphone or camera.

Make Use of the Rule of Thirds: Use the rule of thirds to compose your images by splitting the frame into vertical and horizontal thirds. For aesthetically pleasant photos, put important compositional components along these lines or where they meet.

Seize the Golden Hour Light: Soon after sunrise or before sunset, take advantage of the gentle, warm light to capture breathtaking landscapes and wildlife photographs.

Experiment with Angles: Try a variety of angles and points of view to develop your creative perspective. Try taking pictures from unusual vantage points aboard the ship or low angles for striking landscapes.

Pay Attention to the Details: Take note of the little things that contribute to the distinctiveness of Alaska's fauna and landscapes. Use your camera's or smartphone's macro mode to get up-close pictures of textures, patterns, and intriguing details.

Use HDR Mode for Dynamic Range: If your camera or smartphone has HDR (High Dynamic Range) mode, use it to take pictures of landscapes with a lot of light and shadow, such as woods or glaciers.

Keep Your Camera Steady: To prevent camera shake and guarantee crisp, clear photos, particularly in low light or when using slower shutter speeds, use a tripod or steady your smartphone against a sturdy surface.

Try Out Different Composition Techniques: To give your photos more visual interest, try out various compositional strategies including symmetry, leading lines, and framing.

Capture Wildlife Responsibly: Keep a safe distance and refrain from approaching or upsetting animals when taking pictures of them. To take close-up pictures from a distance, use a telephoto lens or zoom feature.

Accept the Weather: Don't allow bad weather to stop you from capturing pictures. To get dark, atmospheric photos, embrace the dramatic ambiance that rain, fog, or mist creates and make the most of it.

If at all possible, shoot in RAW: To maintain optimal image quality and versatility for post-processing tweaks, shoot in RAW format if your camera or smartphone supports it.

Use Your Photos to Tell a Story: - Utilize your photos to provide a narrative about your Alaskan cruise experience. To produce a visual account of your trip, take pictures of a range of situations, such as sweeping views or unguarded interactions with other passengers.

Try out various compositions and situations, and don't be scared to use your imagination when taking pictures.

Greetings, Readers

I appreciate you joining me on this voyage through the pages of this book. I appreciate your curiosity and excitement for discovering Alaska's breathtaking splendor.

My love of travel and my profound admiration for Alaska's wonders have motivated me to write this guidebook. I've spent a lot of time, money, and energy traveling to this amazing place in order to compile the most accurate and practical information possible to make sure your cruise trip is truly remarkable. Numerous hours of research, firsthand knowledge, and a sincere desire to assist you and your family in making priceless memories are all reflected on each page.

I greatly appreciate your nice review and comments. They are essential in assisting other travelers in finding and using this resource, in addition to validating the effort and commitment put into it. Your remarks have the capacity to uplift and mentor others, improving the travel experiences of many families in the process.

Please think about writing a review and letting us know how this handbook has affected your travels. Your encouragement and comments feed my love of writing and allow me to keep sharing insightful advice with aspiring tourists. By working together, we can guide people to Alaska's treasures and help them embark on their own life-changing experiences.

I appreciate you joining me on this adventure and helping me with my travel guide writing. In addition to giving me encouragement, your glowing review will add to the travel community's overall happiness and exploration.

Sincerely,

Gladys J. Carron

Made in the USA
Monee, IL
15 July 2025